Pebble™ Plus

Dinosaurs and Prehistoric Animals

Velociraptor

by Carol K. Lindeen

Consulting Editor: Gail Saunders-Smith, PhD
Consultant: Jack Horner, Curator of Paleontology
Museum of the Rockies
Bozeman, Montana

Capstone press

Mankato, Minnesota

Pebble Plus is published by Capstone Press,
151 Good Counsel Drive, P.O. Box 669, Mankato, Minnesota 56002.
www.capstonepress.com

1 2 3 4 5 6 10 09 08 07 06 05

Library of Congress Cataloging-in-Publication Data
Lindeen, Carol K., 1976–
    Velociraptor / by Carol K. Lindeen.
    p. cm.—(Pebble plus. Dinosaurs and prehistoric animals)
    Includes bibliographical references and index.
    ISBN 0-7368-4258-6 (hardcover)
    1. Velociraptor—Juvenile literature. I. Title. II. Series.
QE862.S3L497 2006
567.912—dc22   2004026743

Summary: Simple text and illustrations present the life of velociraptors and how they looked and behaved.

Editorial Credits
Sarah L. Schuette, editor; Linda Clavel, set designer; Bobbi J. Dey, book designer; Wanda Winch, photo researcher

Photo and Illustration Credits
Jon Hughes, illustrator
Russell Gooday, 3D Content
Chinasaurus exhibit © Dino Don Inc./Capstone Press/Karon Dubke, 21

Note to Parents and Teachers

The Dinosaurs and Prehistoric Animals set supports national science standards related
to the evolution of life. This book describes and illustrates velociraptors. The images
support early readers in understanding the text. The repetition of words and phrases
helps early readers learn new words. This book also introduces early readers to
subject-specific vocabulary words, which are defined in the Glossary section. Early
readers may need assistance to read some words and to use the Table of Contents,
Glossary, Read More, Internet Sites, and Index sections of the book.

Table of Contents

Fast Dinosaurs

Velociraptors were

fast dinosaurs with feathers.

They ran on two legs.

Velociraptors lived
in prehistoric times.
They lived about 75 million
years ago in Asia.

How Velociraptors Looked

Velociraptors were about
as tall as a large dog.
They were about 3 feet
(1 meter) tall.

Velociraptors had
long heads and flat noses.
They had sharp teeth.

Velociraptors had
stiff tails.
They used their tails
to balance.

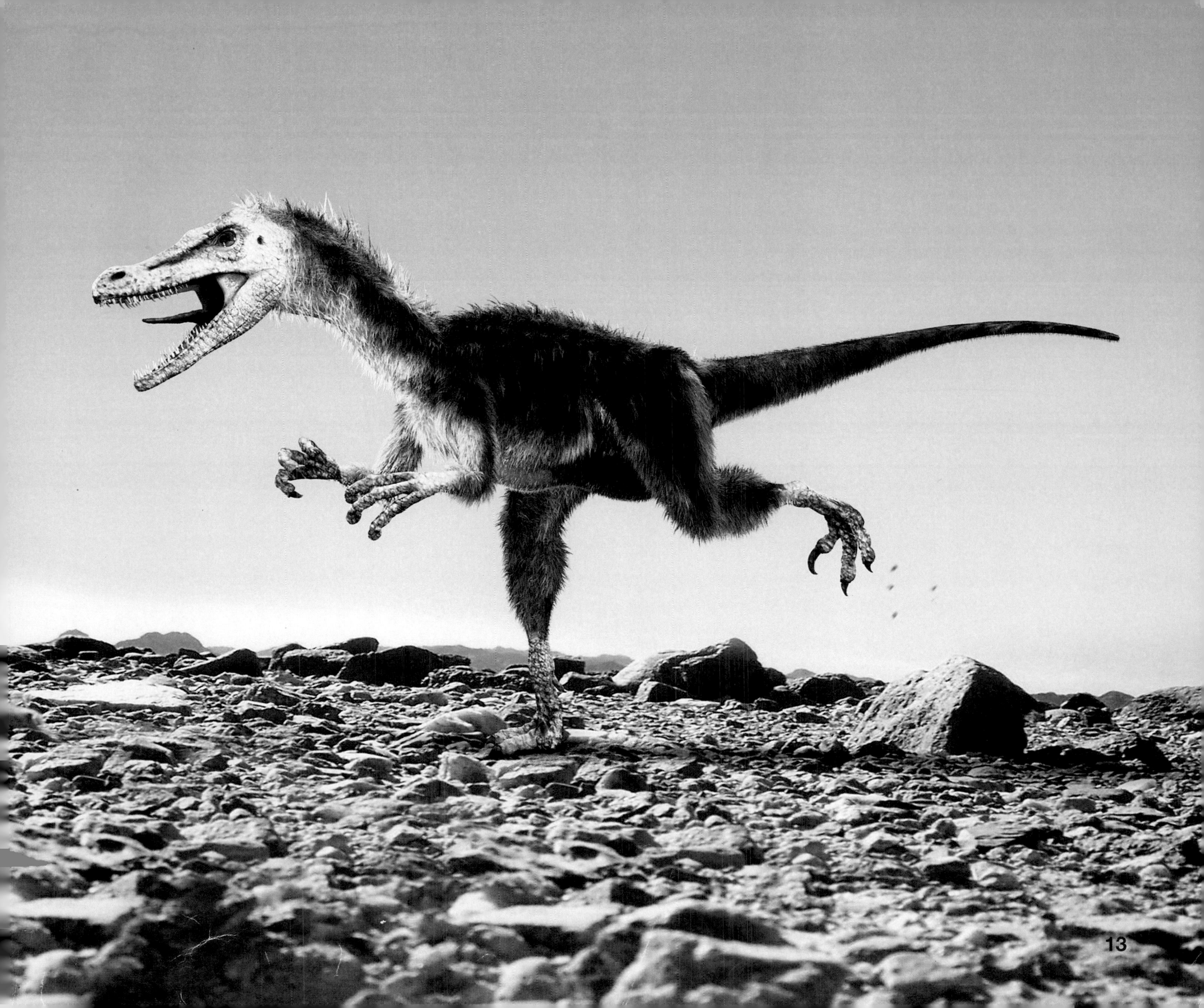

What Velociraptors Did

Velociraptors probably
hunted in groups.
They ate animals
and their eggs.

Velociraptors caught
their prey with sharp claws.
They ripped the prey open.
They swallowed the pieces.

Velociraptors found
dinosaur eggs to eat.
They broke the eggs open
with their sharp teeth.

The End of Velociraptors

The last velociraptors died
about 70 million years ago.
No one knows
why they all died.
You can see velociraptor
fossils in museums.

Glossary

balance—the ability to keep steady and to not fall over

claw—a hard curved nail on the foot of an animal or a bird

dinosaur—a large reptile that lived in prehistoric times

fossil—the remains or traces of an animal or a plant, preserved as rock

hunt—to chase and kill animals for food

museum—a place where objects of art, history, or science are shown

prehistoric—very, very old; prehistoric means belonging to a time before history was written down.

prey—an animal that is hunted for food

Read More

Cohen, Daniel. *Velociraptor.* Discovering Dinosaurs. Mankato, Minn.: Bridgestone Books, 2001.

Dahl, Michael. *Swift Thief: The Adventure of Velociraptor.* Dinosaur World. Minneapolis: Picture Window Books, 2004.

Matthews, Rupert. *Velociraptor.* Gone Forever! Chicago: Heinemann, 2003.

Internet Sites

FactHound offers a safe, fun way to find Internet sites related to this book. All of the sites on FactHound have been researched by our staff.

Here's how:

1. Visit *www.facthound.com*

2. Type in this special code **0736842586** for age-appropriate sites. Or enter a search word related to this book for a more general search.

3. Click on the **Fetch It** button.

FactHound will fetch the best sites for you!

23

Index

Word Count: 128
Grade: 1
Early-Intervention Level: 16